UNSPOKEN WORDS:

THOUGHTS UNFOLD

Gregory Wilkerson

1

Greg Wilkerson

Unspoken Words: Thoughts Unfold

2

Greg Wilkerson

Unspoken Words:

Thoughts Unfold

Gregory Wilkerson

NOAH'S ARK PUBLISHING

3

Greg Wilkerson

Unspoken Words

Noah's Ark Publishing Service
C/o LAVALDREAMS
8549 Wilshire Suite 1442
Beverly Hills, CA 90211

ISBN 978-0-6920695-4-7

4

Greg Wilkerson

Dedication

In loving memory of my father, Gregory Sr., aka "Pretty Boy Floyd."

Unspoken Words: Thoughts Unfold

Greg Wilkerson

Preface

I've been writing ever since I can remember, probably since I was six years old. I was always a different child, getting lost in my thoughts, imagining my future, and often pondering who I'd become when I grew up. It was the passing of my father ten years ago that inspired me to write down my thoughts, whether simple, big, or small. Since his death, writing has been the only thing that has made me whole again. It has allowed me to go back to the place in my thoughts where I used to be as a kid, and it has given me permission to grieve artistically. Writing has taken an unexpected turn for me because I never anticipated actually sharing the thoughts I have kept tucked away.

I remember my father as a very gentle, quiet, and private man who almost never shared his thoughts with many others. I often feel I took on those same characteristics. This book of quotes is simply my thoughts transitioned onto paper and stems from many different emotions and circumstances over a ten-year period. Some of the quotes are simple, some big, and some small. I like to think of some of my quotes as creeds to live by— a little blueprint of this journey we call life. I'm definitely not who I was ten years ago. I've transitioned from being quiet and private to now being willing to share my deepest thoughts. I have

Greg Wilkerson

finally come to the place where I am ready to share my *Unspoken Words*.

"Always say what you mean and mean what you

say so that you are heard clearly with no

confusion."

9

Greg Wilkerson

Greg Wilkerson

"I don't like hand-me-downs.

I don't like the term *lightly used.*

I don't like thrift stores.

I don't like leftover food.

I don't like copies.

I don't like after the fact.

I don't like second best.

Don't count me in any of that."

Greg Wilkerson

12

Greg Wilkerson

"Don't let your need for closure become a burden.

Sometimes the best closure comes from the lesson

learned."

Greg Wilkerson

14

Greg Wilkerson

"Something that was once so close is now so far

from reality. Now you get to admire from afar and

fantasize about your should've, would've, could've.

Sorry won't cut it; that word is like a broken record.

Maybe next time you'll know how to treat someone

with a genuine heart."

Greg Wilkerson

16

Greg Wilkerson

"Be careful with what kind of energy you put into

the universe. You have to be mindful of how you go

about treating people in life. Some people will find

that life has not given them a break. Every time they

turn around they're catching hell. Maybe it's

because karma says you're a scum bag, and scum

bags never win. That's why, when someone does

you wrong, you don't compromise your character;

just let karma do her thing."

Greg Wilkerson

18

Greg Wilkerson

"Know the difference between mad and done. *Mad*

is when you still care and continue to give

emotional energy to the situation. *Done* is when you

are completely over it and no longer feel the need to

have any ties to the situation."

19

Greg Wilkerson

20

Greg Wilkerson

"Re-route, re-vamp, re-coup, but whatever you do, keep going until you get it. You can do it. You will do it. Don't give up. Fight."

21

22

Greg Wilkerson

"When you know someone does not like you for no

real reason, that's a problem that person owns.

Don't spend life internalizing the energy of insecure

people. Smile. Speak. Keep it moving. Protect your

spirit and don't let the internal issues of people

you're around at that job, that meeting, that party,

even that church, compromise your positive energy.

There is nothing to be mad about when you're too

blessed to be stressed."

Greg Wilkerson

24

Greg Wilkerson

"When you're truly secure in who you are, you

simply don't care. Let them internalize and debate

about it."

Greg Wilkerson

26

Greg Wilkerson

"Know your team, know your opponents, know

your friends, know your enemies, know your

promoters, and know your haters, for they are all

important to the outcome of your success."

Greg Wilkerson

28

Greg Wilkerson

"My vibe with every individual is similar to that of
the universe. You will get back what you put out. If
you give me peachy, I feed you peaches. If you give
me hell, well, I'll set your ass on fire."

Greg Wilkerson

30

Greg Wilkerson

"Always respect the heart of those who comes out
and tell you how much they admire you. You never
know what it took for a person to work up enough
courage to do so."

31

Greg Wilkerson

Greg Wilkerson

"When you don't allow breaking to be an option,

you will bounce back even stronger in any aspect of

your life."

Greg Wilkerson

34

Greg Wilkerson

"Prayer must be in the works among all lovers so

that they will feed positivity, compassion,

selflessness, and undying peace to whom their

hearts are connected."

Greg Wilkerson

36

Greg Wilkerson

"Sometimes a tough exterior is worn to protect the warmest hearts. Don't judge the shell."

Greg Wilkerson

38

Greg Wilkerson

"To wear confidence is a sign of peace. Peace in simply being content with yourself and where you are in life at the moment. Many often misconstrue peace when it is made a part of the daily outfit. It's often confused with being mad or upset. Even the silence of peace may often seem intimidating, but there is nothing like peace in knowing who you are, peace in knowing your limitations, peace in knowing your capabilities, and peace in striving to become a better person than you were yesterday."

Greg Wilkerson

40

Greg Wilkerson

"Many are often confused by the act of being sexy.

There are two key components that make a person

sexy. First, that person is highly desirable, and

second, he or she manages to maintain his or her

suspense. Being known for going from bedpost to

bedpost never made anyone sexy. That just simply

makes that person busy."

Greg Wilkerson

42

Greg Wilkerson

"You'll find that most people who embrace staying

in their lane do so with a smile. It is a defense

mechanism against pointless exposure to negative

energy. Very seldom is a major highway

intertwined with a dead end."

Greg Wilkerson

44

Greg Wilkerson

"I've never believed the old saying that goes, 'You

are who you're with," because a strong-minded

individual will not be easily influenced. In your

search for friends, seek loyal, down-to-earth

individuals, and people who are real. Care less

about titles, social status, or what a person does in

his or her spare time. If we're friends, I accept you

for who you are—no judgement, with open arms.

There is only one condition: I expect the same."

Greg Wilkerson

46

Greg Wilkerson

"Always be the best *you*. You never know who you

are shaking hands with. Opportunities can come

from the most unexpected places, and it's not

always about what you know, but who you know."

Greg Wilkerson

48

Greg Wilkerson

"Some of the most intelligent, successful people in

the world hardly ever wear a suit."

49

Greg Wilkerson

50

Greg Wilkerson

"You don't have to feature yourself on the scene of everything you hear about yourself. People who are on a mission don't make time to be distracted by what others are saying that's not conducive to promoting their destiny."

51

Greg Wilkerson

52

Greg Wilkerson

"In life, many faces will offer you many invitations.

Be wise enough to know which are worth your

attendance."

Greg Wilkerson

54

Greg Wilkerson

"Being misunderstood comes with the territory of

greatness and perseverance. Educate more. Take

things personal less."

Greg Wilkerson

56

Greg Wilkerson

"When you possess standards and know what you

have to offer, you are content with those moments

of living single. It gives you time to be particular

about whom and what you bring into your life. A

loose person will not understand this concept."

Greg Wilkerson

58

Greg Wilkerson

"Be mindful of the image you allow your tongue to

create for you while fabricating the image of

someone else. Character always speaks louder than

words."

Greg Wilkerson

60

Greg Wilkerson

"Some will try too hard to be seen, but be intimated

by someone else's natural glow. Natural character

will always speak for itself. When you truly have it,

you don't have to draw it on, paste it on, or glam it

up. Your shine will simply be inevitable."

Greg Wilkerson

62

Greg Wilkerson

"You're either for me or against me. The most

dangerous people are the ones who linger around in

your life and straddle the fence."

Greg Wilkerson

64

Greg Wilkerson

"Always be aware of the difference between who

wants to be with you and who wants to be you."

65

Greg Wilkerson

66

Greg Wilkerson

"Inconsistency and lack of communication is a no-win situation. Secure people do not play the game of cat & mouse, and will refuse the chase. Now, what they do play is a mean hand in a game called 'Next!'"

Greg Wilkerson

Greg Wilkerson

"Never take the time out of your life to address anything or anyone that's irrelevant to your well-being. People know when you have surrendered the power to make them relevant: when you entertain their shenanigans. So laugh and enjoy their "fool's show." You are so much bigger than their production."

69

Greg Wilkerson

Unspoken Words: Thoughts Unfold

70

Greg Wilkerson

"If it's not about Jesus or money, don't bother me

with the mess. I've had my share of heartache and

pains. Don't go adding more to my test. Like a lily

in a valley shining at my best, yes, indeed, I'm

blessed. Don't you think it's time I rest?"

Greg Wilkerson

72

Greg Wilkerson

"There are two types of questions: those that are

asked out of pure curiosity and those that are asked

due to discernment. Anyone with a true, discerning

spirit has already discovered the evidence and

confirmed the answer before the approach. They are

just in hopes that there isn't a lie told."

Greg Wilkerson

74

Greg Wilkerson

"Invest in yourself and your future so that you can

have more of your time and less time on their

clock."

Greg Wilkerson

76

Greg Wilkerson

"There is a higher power among us, and He will place us right where we need to be to get us where we desire to go. Be grateful for all the signs and affirmations He reveals to bring our journey into perspective. His presence sustains every step of the way as guidance."

Greg Wilkerson

Greg Wilkerson

"Wait on God to send someone special in your life

because, when you wait on the Lord for your gift,

you'll find that He doesn't give lying gifts, cheating

gifts, ugly gifts, or broke gifts."

Greg Wilkerson

Greg Wilkerson

"When life puts you in a position where there is no

sorrow, that is a sign indicating that you are at the

place you're supposed to be. It's called your

blessing. Don't miss out on it worrying about

somebody else's spot. You don't know what he or

she is going through to keep it."

Greg Wilkerson

82

Greg Wilkerson

"If you're somewhere and the energy feels off, and

you just can't seem to put your finger on why, that

is called discerning energy. Feel it. Hear it.

Sometimes it creeps in slowly, like a whisper. Other

times it's a loud yell, saying run like hell. Just do

what it says. The rationale will be revealed later."

83

Greg Wilkerson

84

Greg Wilkerson

"Be smart. Be pretty. Be successful. But be wise enough to know that you may not be someone's type. Don't feel inadequate. Don't lose confidence. Find peace in knowing that you will be glad in what is meant just for you, and know that it will be well worth your wait."

Greg Wilkerson

86

Greg Wilkerson

"Feeling sorry for someone is not a love life. If

you're going to help out a friend, do so from the

heart and tell them "may God bless" as you see

them on their journey, because obviously they have

work to do. This will prevent less heartache and

confusion in life."

87

Greg Wilkerson

Greg Wilkerson

"Some people are like a hot eye on a stove. When they've made contact and realized it burned, only a fool reaches back in and touches the eye again."

89

Greg Wilkerson

90

Greg Wilkerson

"The best way to get the attention of a guy or girl

you like is by always showing up cute and ignore

them."

Greg Wilkerson

Greg Wilkerson

"Excellence is achieved most often due to someone

operating out of fear but deciding to go in anyway."

Greg Wilkerson

94

Greg Wilkerson

"Don't spend too much of your life worrying.

Whatever is meant for you will simply come into

existence when it is time. Instead, focus on being

the best you can possibly be, and the best

connections, opportunities, and relationships will

appear inevitably."

Greg Wilkerson

96

Greg Wilkerson

"Never allow anyone to make you feel guilty about possessing anything you've worked hard for. We serve a mighty God who is a miracle worker of all things, and He is not poor."

Greg Wilkerson

98

Greg Wilkerson

"Sometimes you just have to go in there, be

fearless, and think more about the possibility of

everything working out and less about the what-ifs."

Greg Wilkerson

100

Greg Wilkerson

"A positive attitude will take you a long way, even

when it comes to love interests. Believe it or not,

there are people who don't put up with cute

people's crap either."

Greg Wilkerson

102

Greg Wilkerson

"Never let what people say ruin things for you.

Learn how to do you. Do you so well, with such

class and grace, that even your shade looks

confusing."

103

Greg Wilkerson

104

Greg Wilkerson

"Life may keep you busy, but allow time to grieve,

even if you have to grieve on the go."

105

Greg Wilkerson

106

Greg Wilkerson

"Over and over the words play in my mind, the ones

I last spoke, not knowing your shortage of time.

Frustrated with the inability to un-live the moment

is killing me. "I love you." "I'll see you tomorrow."

The words confidently rolled off my tongue, but I

didn't know that the day would never even come."

Greg Wilkerson

Greg Wilkerson

Biography

Gregory Wilkerson Jr., is a native of Jacksonville, Florida, and a high school graduate of Douglas Anderson School of Arts. He later completed his undergraduate studies at the University of Central Florida, followed by graduate studies at Grand Canyon University. Gregory enjoys writing and plans to continue strengthening his craft.

Greg Wilkerson

Unspoken Words: Thoughts Unfold

Contact the Author

Myunspokenwords50@gmail.com

Contact the Publisher

noahsarkpublishing@gmail.com

www.lavaldreams.com

Greg Wilkerson

Made in the USA
Columbia, SC
18 April 2023

15559073R00061